# WARNING!
# PUBLIC SCHOOLS
# AREN'T FOR CHRISTIANS!

## A BIBLICAL PERSPECTIVE

BY
RICHARD "LITTLE BEAR" WHEELER

PUBLISHED BY
MANTLE MINISTRIES PRESS
228 STILL RIDGE
BULVERDE, TEXAS 78163

Dedicated to my Saviour and Lord, Who
has kept me these many years,
and has given me a the gift of
a truly wonderful wife, Marilyn,
and children,
Noelle, Aimee, and Joshua.
To my dearest friends:
thank you for your love,
encouragement,
and support.


Special thanks to editors
Rick Townsend, Carol Blair,
and my wife, Marilyn, and
to Don Salter for computer layout.

# Table of Contents

**Warning!** This book deals with a delicate subject—the dangers of government education in America. Below is a list of subjects that are addressed from a Biblical perspective. If you use even one of the six reasons as justification for placing your children in a public school, this book is a "must" reading.

1. We do not really want to place our children in a public school, but we are in a financial crunch and there are no other alternatives.

2. The real world is full of sinners; therefore, I need to place my children in the public school system to help them cope with real situations that arise in life.

3. I keep my children in public schools because I want them to be, as the Bible says, "salt and light"—and to be a Godly example to the lost around them. Isn't this what Christ has commanded us to do?

4. My son/daughter loves sports, and the public schools offer the best programs. This is why I allow my children to go to public schools.

5. I do not feel qualified to teach my children at home, and I cannot afford a Christian school; therefore, I have no choice but to place my children in a public school.

6. Look at me! I made it through the public school system and turned out all right, so I am sure my children will turn out OK in the end.

# PREFACE

My goal in this booklet is to compile a list of Biblical passages and prove by the use of Scripture that a godless school system is abhorrent to the will of God. This book is not intended to be an exhaustive treatment of the dangers of godless government schools, as there are many well-written books on the subject of the damage caused by the current American government system of education. It will take courage for committed government-school devotees to read this book. The book will make most government school officials fuming mad. Many Christian parents, and perhaps some church leaders, will dismiss this work as that of a fanatic. Perhaps this is because many people have made public schools their "sacred cow."

It is the nature of carnal man to want to go back to Egypt and to resurrect familiar idols that have become a part of our old natures. This is visibly seen in Exodus Chapter 32. This portion of Scripture contains the well-known account of Moses returning from Mount Sinai with the tablets of stone. Upon his return, he found Aaron leading the children of Israel in the sin of idolatry before their sacred cow. In reacting to this passage many Christians often say, "How could these people have been so stupid? I would never have done that!"

Remember that people born under the old sin nature have a propensity to do that which is wrong—not right. Another human tendency is to do that which is most familiar. Bad habits are always easy to learn and hard to break. After all, the parents reason, "We went to the *Egyptian schools* (so to speak), and they didn't do *us* any harm, so how could they hurt our children?" What I am inferring is that once a Christian has been set free from the bondage of sin by the work of Christ on the cross, the parents who enroll their children in government schools are dooming their children to the idiolatry from which they themselves have been fortunate to escape. The average Christian parent cannot imagine the damage a government school can cause in young minds.

I challenge you as a parent, grandparent, or church leader,

to read this book and pray that God will open your understanding. Examine the Biblical conclusions and try to disprove them. I do not stand alone in warning parents to keep their children out of government schools.

Martin Luther warned parents about schools over four centuries ago. His warning is as relevant today as it was then:

> *"I am much afraid that schools will prove to be the gates of hell unless they diligently labor in explaining the Holy Scriptures, engraving them in the hearts of youth.* **I advise no one to place their child where the Scriptures do not reign paramount. Every institution in which men are not increasingly occupied with the word of God must become corrupt.** *"* Martin Luther, A.D.1537

The only justifiable basis for Christian parents to send their children to the current tax-supported government school system is that the school is teaching Biblical principles and is dedicated in training youth in not only an education of knowledge, but far more importantly, an education in wisdom—which can be derived only from the study of the Bible and imparted by the Holy Spirit. Obviously, the public schools are not doing this!

Compare the goals of today's government schools with New York state's former goals, as described by New York's first public school principal, who served from 1810-1848:

> *"The faithful teacher enjoys the approval of Heaven. He is employed, if he has the right spirit, in a Heavenly Father's business that man should be made wiser and happier. To this end, the Son of God, the Great Teacher, came to bless our race; so far as the schoolmaster has the spirit of Jesus, he is engaged in the same great work.*
>
> *"Very justly, we attribute our superiority as a people over those who dwell in the darker portions of the world, to our purer faith, derived from that precious fountain of truth, the Bible. In our public schools, supported at the public expense, and in which the children of all denominations meet for instruction, I do not think that any man has a right to crowd his*

*own peculiar notions of a theology upon all, whether they are acceptable or not. Yet there is a common ground which he can occupy. He can teach a reverence for a Supreme Being, a reverence for the Word of God, for the influence of His Spirit, for the character and teachings of our Savior. For the momentous concerns of eternity, he can teach the duty of repentance, and the privileges of forgiveness, and the salvation by His Son."* David Perkins Page

You can see from the above quotation, as with the proverbial frog slowly boiling in the pot, our government has boiled the American people into a state of blindness and made them believe that the education of their children is like it was in the "good old days." Even the schools of the '50s and '60s that many of us parents attended were already heading down the slippery road to corruption. When the Ten Commandments and school prayer were replaced with the religion of secular humanism, the schools' demise was predictable—as Martin Luther wrote. By failing to honor God and expelling Him from the schools, we have hurt our children and incurred God's displeasure on our nation.

*"Wherefore the LORD God of Israel saith, I said indeed that thy house, and the house of thy father, should walk before me forever; but now the LORD saith, Be it far from me; for them that honour me I will honour, and they that despise me shall be lightly esteemed"* (I Samuel 2:30).

I am sure that some parents think they have extenuating circumstances and are hard pressed for any other alternatives to government schools. However, Jesus challenged those committed to Him to walk in faith in all areas of life. The bottom line is, "Are you as a parent sure that you have received the blessing of God to send your children to the government public schools, which are determined to destroy the Christian faith of children? The same schools that have politically expelled Christ and His Word from the classroom?" The tragedy is, though, that 85% of evangelical Christians are dedicated to sending their offspring to these truly Biblically incorrect schools. This is beyond belief. Parents are either willfully sinning or blindly ignorant in allowing the godless government we have in America today to raise their children. Either way, ignorance will exact a very high price. Ignorance is *not* bliss, but rather the first installment toward moral bankruptcy.

*"Be not deceived, God is not mocked: for whatsoever a man soweth, that shall he also reap. For he that soweth to his flesh shall of the flesh reap corruption; but he that soweth to the Spirit shall of the Spirit reap life everlasting. And let us not be weary in well doing; for in due season we shall reap, if we faint not" (Galatians 6:7-9).*

Below are two definitions of education. The first is the current altered version of Noah Webster's dictionary. The second is taken from the original 1828 Noah Webster dictionary. As you read, take note of the differences in the purpose of education then and now, and see how far the American school system has drifted from our nation's early intentions. We have changed so much, that in order to fit the current corrupt system of education we have had to re-work the definition into a "politically correct" modern version.

### Modern definition:

*"Education is the act or process of imparting or acquiring general knowledge and of developing the powers of reasoning and judgment. The act or process of imparting or acquiring particular knowledge or skills, as for a profession."*

### Original definition:

*"Education is the bringing up, as a child; instruction; formation of manners. Education comprehends all that series of instruction and discipline, which is intended to enlighten the understanding, correct the temper, and form the manners and habits of youth, and fit them for usefulness in their future stations. To give children a good education in manners, arts, and science, is important; to give them a religious education is indispensable; and an immense responsibility rests on parents and guardians who neglect these duties."*

The most important element of education is the religious instruction that Noah Webster had the boldness to include in his definition. Along with his definition he admonished parents not to neglect their responsibility to educate their children themselves or else to delegate that education to other Godly authorities.

The pity of giving children to the government to educate is that the government is dedicated to fostering atheism and relativism. Many parents will reply, "I came through the system all right," or "I know many students who have not lost their faith." The question parents need to consider is this: "Do you want to play Russian roulette with your children?"

For every success story there are countless other accounts of shipwrecked children who have lost their zeal for the Lord and have conformed to the standards of their peers. Satan is a clever devil. He will allow some "wheat" to come through the system so as to deceive the blinded parents as to the real nature of godless government education.

The bottom line is this: **"What does the Bible have to say on the matter?"** With this question, you cannot get angry at me or at anyone else who will challenge your right to send your children to government schools.

By the way, are our children, *our* children, or are we *stewards* of our children? God desires that our children be raised for His glory. Christian parents need to ask, "Does the current educational system in government schools accomplish the task of preparing children to be useful for the Lord?"

Can you imagine what God would have done if the Israelites had sent their children to the Philistines or the Egyptians for their education? Then why do Christian parents continue to send their children to schools dedicated to the destruction of their minds and morals? Another question to consider is this: "If Christ were visibly walking among us today and we could ask Him directly if we should place our Christian children in the atheistic government schools of America, how do you suppose He would reply?"

# LEST WE FORGET

## IF THE FOUNDATIONS BE DESTROYED
## Psalm 11:3

*"If the foundations be destroyed, what can the righteous do?" (Psalm 11:3).*

There are reasons for the deterioration of anything in life, and the most obvious reason is *neglect.* It is not that people want to have the results of neglect in their lives, it is just that in the busyness of life, untended problems take their toll. When my father-in-law was living, he owned a ten-unit apartment building, and I noticed how he constantly spent time maintaining the apartments. He never let even minor problems escape his watchful eye. I learned many valuable lessons over the years from observing him and helping him maintain that building.

In a similar manner, parents must maintain high educational standards for the sake of their children. It is amazing how decayed and fallen the educational system of America has become. In the last 35 years, the Christian educational foundations established by our Founding Fathers have been tragically destroyed.

### HARVARD UNIVERSITY:

In 1636, Clergyman John Harvard contributed his personal library and property for the founding of the first college in America, in Cambridge, Massachusetts. Within 16 years of the landing of the Pilgrims, America had a college "to train a literate clergy." Rules and precepts for the school's charter were formulated on September 26, 1642. They stated in part (original spelling retained):

1

*"Let every student be plainly instructed, and earnestly pressed to consider well, the maine end of his life and studies is, to know God and Jesus Christ which is eternall life, John 17:3 and therefore to lay Christ in the bottome, as the only foundation of all sound knowledge and learning. And seeing the Lord only giveth wisedome, Let every one seriously set himself by prayer in secret to seeke it of Him."*

## THE OLD DELUDER SATAN LAW:

Shortly after Harvard was established, the colonists of Massachusetts and Connecticut wanted the children of their respective colonies to be educated in order not to remain ignorant of Christian self-government, nor to lack the ability to govern themselves according to God's Word. The leaders of Massachusetts and Connecticut passed the "Old Deluder Satan Law" in 1647. This law stated:

*"It being one chiefe project of that old deluder, Satan, to keepe men from the knowledge of the scriptures, as in former time....It is therefore ordered.....[that] after the Lord hath increased [the settlement] to the number of fifty howshoulders, [they] shall forthwith appoint one within theire towne, to teach all such children as shall resorte to him, to write and read . . . and it is further ordered, That where any towne shall increase to the number of one hundred families or howshoulders, they shall sett up a grammar schoole for the university."*

## WILLIAM AND MARY COLLEGE:

William and Mary was founded in 1693 in Williamsburg, Virginia, through the vision of Reverend James Blair. The seminary-college became the home of education for many of the Founding Fathers of America. Men such as George

Washington, Benjamin Franklin, Thomas Jefferson, James Monroe, George Wythe, John Tyler, John Marshall, and sixteen members of the Continental Congress studied there. The school's charter, drawn up in 1693, stated the goals and purposes of the college:

"William and Mary, by the grace of God, of England, Scotland, France and Ireland, King and Queen, Defenders of the faith, to all whom these our present Letters shall come, greeting.

*'Forasmuch as our well-beloved and trusty subjects, constituting the General Assembly of our Colony of Virginia, have had it in their minds, and have proposed to themselves, to the end that the Church of Virginia may be furnished with a Seminary of Ministers of the Gospel, and that the youth may be piously educated in Good Letters and Manners, and that the Christian Faith may be propagated amongst the Western Indians, to the glory of God.'"*

### YALE UNIVERSITY:

In 1701 a Collegiate School at Saybrook, Connecticut, was started by ten Congregational ministers. The school was later moved to New Haven, Connecticut, and renamed *Yale* in honor of Mr. Elihu Yale, an American-born English merchant and governor of the East India Company. Mr. Yale donated books and materials from his fortune, totaling $2,800—a considerable sum for those days. He was instrumental in shaping the college bylaws, which stated the chief aim of education:

*"Every student shall consider the main end of his study, to wit, to know God in Jesus Christ and answerably to lead a Godly, sober life."*

## PRINCETON UNIVERSITY:

Princeton was originally called "The College of New Jersey" and was located in Princeton, New Jersey. Over the years the name was simplified to *Princeton.* Like all of America's early colleges, the school was established to train young men in *"God's Holy Word and to become a useful ordainment to society."* The sentiment of America's educators is seen in this quote by Princeton's first president, Rev. Jonathan Dickinson.

*"Cursed be all that learning that is contrary to the cross of Christ."*

I wonder what Rev. Dickinson would think of America's educational system today. I shudder to think what he would think of the fact that the majority of Christian parents place their children in the schools as they stand today. You can see that America's early schools were intended strictly for the propagation of Christian principles and the refinement of the character of sinful man. Our Founding Fathers realized that America would be successful only if its citizens were a religious and moral people. They also knew that they must establish Godly schools in order to educate youth to control sinful passions by the reading of God's Word, the Bible. While President of the United States (1801-1809), Thomas Jefferson chaired the school board for the District of Columbia, where he wrote the first plan of education adopted by the city of Washington. That plan used the Bible and Isaac Watts' hymnal as the principal books for teaching reading. His sentiments were as follows:

*"The Christian Religion, when divested of the rags in which they [the clergy] have enveloped it, and brought to the original*

*purity and simplicity of its benevolent institutor, is a religion of all others most friendly to liberty, science, and the freest expansion of the human mind."*

The obvious deterioration of a nation is caused by the removal of God's principles, contained in His Word, the Bible. Even a passing study of Israel's forsaking of God's commandments will bear out this truth. America is foolishly heading down the same road that Israel traveled in forsaking God. Note the blatant violations that have transpired in the past 100 years, and weep for this nation. On June 25, 1962, the Supreme Court declared in *Engel v. Vitale* that it was unconstitutional to use the Bible in government schools, that,

*"A wall of separation between church and state exists."*

That disastrous decision opened a "Pandora's box" of attacks on Christian values in the government schools of this once-Godly land. The following summer, on June 17, 1963, the same Court ruled on the case of *Abington v. Schempp* and stated:

*"If portions of the New Testament were read without explanation, they could be . . . psychologically harmful to the child."*

In *Stone v. Graham* in 1980, the Supreme Court ruled that the Ten Commandments, which for centuries had been held in the highest honor by nations and various religions of the world, could no longer be placed on the government school walls of America. The Court said:

*"If posted copies of the Ten Commandments are to have any effect at all, it will be to induce the school children to read, meditate upon, and perhaps to venerate and obey the Commandments. . . . This is not permissible. . . ."*

# THE BIBLE AND EDUCATION

## IT TAKES A FAMILY
### Proverbs 1:8-9

Mrs. Hillary Clinton wrote a book entitled *It Takes a Village*. The book falsely asserts that America's children need to be raised primarily by the community—a line of thinking prevalent in America today. Because of higher learning we have become a nation that believes that the "professionals" can do a better job than the parents. This idea is a great deception—especially for Christian parents. The Bible tells us that the instruction of children is the **responsibility of the parents.**

*"My son, hear the instruction of thy father, and forsake not the law of thy mother; For they shall be an ornament of grace unto thy head, and chains about thy neck" (Proverbs 1:8-9).*

The above Scripture does not say that the primary instruction should be left to government school officials, or the "village," but to the parent. If however, you choose to relegate your God-given responsibility, make sure that those you allow to teach your children are Godly and that the curriculum is Christ-centered—producing Christian virtues in the children which will then be "ornaments of grace."

Many Christian parents seem fearful that they do not have the intelligence to teach their children. The Bible declares that God *"shall supply all your needs" (Philippians 4:19).* Only recently have parents delegated the primary teaching of their children to others. Look back into history. Here are just a few of those who were taught primarily by their parents and relatives: Pilgrim Governor William Bradford, Jonathan Edwards, John and Charles Wesley, Wolfgang Mozart, George and Martha Washington, John Quincy Adams, Abraham Lincoln, Robert E. Lee, Florence Nightingale, and Woodrow Wilson.

The primary goal of the parent is to teach Godly, Christ-centered character, and this is something that all Christian parents can do. The ability to transmit knowledge will vary with parents' ability and educational background. In my experience, knowledge has come with maturity. Even relatively poorly educated parents, however, can take today's excellent curricula and learn together with their children. So the perceived weakness can be turned into a strength, as the students and parents learn together. You really *can* do this with your children!! In some ways, it becomes more fun for the children, as they become co-learners with their parents. And there is no better way to learn something than to teach it. But consider the danger of knowledge apart from Christ-like character. If this situation occurs, the result is frequently that the person only becomes a more clever devil. This is precisely the type of knowledge that is being imparted to young children in the godless government schools of America today.

The Bible says that the "natural man" (unsaved) does not understand the things of God. Why? Because the things of God are foolishness to him or her since he or she does not have the spiritual eyes received only when one is born again. I Corinthians Chapter 2, clearly shows that the wisdom of God is far superior to the knowledge of this world. According to God's Word, it is these eternal spiritual truths which parents have the responsibility to teach. However, government schools will not allow these essentials to be taught. Indeed, in the godless system currently in place, it would be impossible for the schools to do so.

The majority of Americans have mistakenly made the quest for higher learning the equivalent of an idol. Consider how often even Christian people will ask young people, "Where do you plan to go to college," or "What profession do you plan to follow?" Perhaps better questions would be, "What has the Lord been showing you lately?" or, "Where do you believe the Lord may be calling you to serve Him?"

It is amazing to think that the Israelites left Egypt with all its fancy systems of knowledge and its many conveniences of the day, in order to be intentionally led into the wilderness where there were no schools or market places. Perhaps the Lord had to deprogram Israel from the humanistic elements they had adopted while living in Egypt for more than four hundred years. Perhaps the Lord wanted to teach Israel that they needed to be completely dependent on Him, rather than on the Egyptian form of government and society.

A major problem with education apart from God is that it creates in the student a false sense of self-sufficiency and independence. It enables the student to believe he can provide everything he needs for himself. Now, think this through. Is that what God desires? Or does He desire us to be completely dependent on Him for His manna? The impression I get from reading the Bible is that the Lord delights in those who lean upon Him and feel utterly helpless. Even continued higher education is not an end unto itself, but only a tool that the Lord can use if He deems it necessary to accomplish His goals and purposes on behalf of those who yield to His leading. Think of all the Christian people you know, and consider what they studied in all their years of schooling. How often is this education the source of their current livelihood? In my experience, it seems that the majority of people have been led into completely different professions from what they pursued in college.

By way of testimony, I was what school officials today might call a "late bloomer." The report cards I received had notes on the back for my parents to read, such as, "Your son is retarded." They invented remedial reading programs to help me, but these were of no avail. The Roman Catholic schools in those days used corporal punishment to train students how to learn. In my case, they broke sticks over my knuckles and twisted my ears until I was sure they would be removed completely. The sisters literally tried to shake sense into me and flunked me to improve my plight, but none of this worked. I did not learn to read, spell, or write until I was in the sixth grade at twelve years of age. By the twelfth grade, in spite of public and private education, I caught up to my senior graduating class and graduated as an average student.

During these trying days I had only one strength, and that was my faith in the Lord Jesus. I was convinced that someday, He would use me for His glory, in spite of my being "retarded." This He has indeed done. Today, some forty years later, I can say that the Lord has blessed me abundantly and has prospered me beyond my own expectations. (Ephesians 3:20)

As I look back over my early schooling, I can honestly say, as I am sure you too will admit, I have learned more outside of school then I ever learned in school. Besides some useful skills I learned in school, I now find I have additional things which I would be better off "unlearning," by the renewing of my mind through God's Word. Therefore, Christian parents are far more qualified than unredeemed "professionals" to instruct their children in what really matters most in life. In most cases, all they lack is the desire and commitment to follow God in this endeavor, as you will discover, as I urge you to read on.

## WE'VE GOT YOU COVERED
### Isaiah 40:11

*"He shall feed his flock like a shepherd: he shall gather the lambs with his arm, and carry them in his bosom, and shall gently lead those that are with young" (Isaiah 40:11).*

Are you like a shepherd carrying your children in your bosom of protection from the wolf—Satan—who wants to devour them? One of my favorite expressions I recall while viewing those old corny 1950's cowboy, gunfighter westerns on T.V. is the expression, "I've got you covered." Remember the scenario? The two "good guys" wearing white hats were trying to drive out the "bad guys" wearing black hats from the old farmhouse. They edge their way ever so close under murderous gunfire, with Hollywood six shooters that never run out of bullets. The good guy says to his buddy as he makes a dangerous and desperate attempt to cross open ground to get to the large boulder closer to the farmhouse, "Run! I've got you covered!" He tears out, shooting as he goes, while his buddy is pouring lead as fast as he can into the windows of the farm house to protect his buddy during his dangerous exposure.

This example is exactly as it should be with parents toward their children. Obviously the "bad guy" is Satan and his demons trying to destroy children. The job of the parent is to keep them "under cover." All of this deals with what the Bible calls *authority.* As I began to do a Bible study on the word *authority,* I discovered some deep truth that has impacted my life and my children for the better. I found that there is power in authority. The power is for both good and evil, depending upon who is wielding the authority at the time. A Biblical example of this is

seen in the following text involving Christ while exercising His
authority over Satan:

*"And they went into Capernaum; and straightway on the
sabbath day he entered into the synagogue, and taught. And
they were astonished at his doctrine: for he taught them as one
that had authority, and not as the scribes. And there was in
their synagogue a man with an unclean spirit; and he cried out,
Saying, Let us alone; what have we to do with thee, thou Jesus
of Nazareth? art thou come to destroy us? I know thee who thou
art, the Holy One of God. And Jesus rebuked him, saying, Hold
thy peace, and come out of him. And when the unclean spirit
had torn him, and cried with a loud voice, he came out of him.
And they were all amazed, insomuch that they questioned
among themselves, saying, What thing is this? what new
doctrine is this? for with **authority** commandeth he even the
unclean spirits, and they do obey him" (Mark 1:21-27).*

Here you see the power of authority to heal and to set free.
The power of authority was used for good.

Satan also carries the power of authority for evil and
destructive purposes. In Luke Chapter 4, we see Satan trying to
use his authority to get Jesus to submit to his control:

*"And the devil said unto him, all this **power** will I give thee,
and the glory of them: for that is delivered unto me; and to
whomsoever I will, I give it. If thou therefore wilt worship me,
all shall be thine" (Luke 4:6-7).*

The understanding of authority is essential in raising our
children and living our daily lives. Yet, so few understand its
implications. Even Jesus was surprised when he met a man
outside of the house of Israel who understood the power of
authority. This encounter was recorded in Matthew 8:5-13:

*"And when Jesus was entered into Capernaum, there came
unto him a centurion, beseeching him, And saying, Lord, my*

*servant lieth at home sick of the palsy, grievously tormented.
And Jesus saith unto him, I will come and heal him. The
centurion answered and said, Lord, I am not worthy that thou
shouldest come under my roof: but speak the word only, and my
servant shall be healed. For I am a man under **authority**,
having soldiers under me: and I say to this man, Go, and he
goeth; and to another, Come, and he cometh; and to my
servant, Do this, and he doeth it. When Jesus heard it, he
marvelled, and said to them that followed, Verily I say unto
you, I have not found so great faith, no, not in Israel. And I say
unto you, That many shall come from the east and west, and
shall sit down with Abraham, and Isaac, and Jacob, in the
kingdom of heaven. But the children of the kingdom shall be
cast out into outer darkness: there shall be weeping and
gnashing of teeth. And Jesus said unto the centurion, Go thy
way; and as thou hast believed, so be it done unto thee. And his
servant was healed in the selfsame hour."*

This centurion understood the ramifications and power of
authority. His understanding of the authority of Christ, coupled
with his faith and the power to speak authority into action,
accomplished the healing of his servant. After my Scriptural
study of authority, I began to see that authority can be
transferred to accomplish both good and evil, and that nothing
is neutral. In other words, whenever we or our children sit under
instruction, view television, see a video, listen to music, read a
book, or engage in numerous other activities, the power of
authority is present to change the behavior of those under its
sway for both good and evil—depending upon what is being
submitted to.

If this is the case, when parents send their children to
godless government schools, the children are placed under
someone else's authority and power. If the teacher happens to

be a homosexual, he is transferring the power of his lifestyle to the innocent minds of children. The teacher may or may not be up-front with his lifestyle, but his world view is tainted to reflect his devious behavior, regardless, and his authority carries power in his spoken words to alter the minds of those under his teachings.

When you send your child anywhere outside your authority, it is your responsibility to see that you have him or her "covered." I cannot begin to tell you in this limited space of the tragic stories recounted to me from parents all over this nation who have testified of the damage that has occurred to their precious children when they have ignorantly given up their authority to protect their children. You would be amazed where their children were when they were wounded, and in some cases destroyed. One mother recounted how her seven-year-old son was violated at a family member's home. A Christian father told me about the witchcraft involvement his daughter was exposed to while at a slumber party at a *Christian* friend's home *while the hosting parents were home.* A twelve-year-old boy told me of the nudity he viewed on his friend's VCR while the friend's mother was in the other room. One Christian mother told me of her Godly Christian teen daughter who fell away from the Lord because of the influences of rebellious government educated peers at work, and her introduction to hideous rock music after hours. While pastoring some years ago, I had the unpleasant duty to inform some dear friends that their Christian son was using drugs at public school. The list goes on and on.

I warn parents that when their child leaves their presence, they had better delegate their authority to proper God-given channels. Using my former example of the old westerns, it would be like the parents who run out of bullets while covering their children as they run from one place to the other. If the parents are out of bullets, they had better make sure that there are others keeping the children under cover while the parent reloads. In like manner, sending children into a godless government school is not only not covering them with God-ordained proper authority, it is as foolish as sending their children into the farmhouse where the bad guys are. By the time the parents reload and their children return home after school, they have already been shot full of the "holes" of being taught lies and deception all day.

One of the major deceptions parents are under is the idea that the current government elementary school system is basically neutral and teaches the important skills of writing, reading, and arithmetic. However, after the subtle erosion of twelve years of humanism, the damage is often not seen until it is too late. And it is most often not until the teenage years that the damage becomes apparent.

## BEWARE OF FOOLS
### Psalm 14:1

*"The fool hath said in his heart, 'There is no God.' They are corrupt, they have done abominable works, there is none that doeth good" (Psalm 14:1).*

The word for "fool" in the Bible is a very strong word and carries with it the injunction not to even give the time of day to such a person. Yet in America, Christian parents send their children to classrooms to receive instruction from educated fools—who say in their hearts and minds, "There is no God." Fools who teach godless history, sex education, and evolutionary science.

14

*"O LORD, how great are thy works! And thy thoughts are very deep. A [foolish] man knoweth not; neither doth a fool understand this" (Psalm 92:5-6).*

The conclusion of the above Scripture is that in the present government schools throughout America, those in authority have established a policy not to teach the "works and thoughts of God." Therefore, the system is being run by foolish men and women and is destined to bear the fruit of their foolishness, as we can easily observe. No wonder many students now graduate with a third-grade reading level.

With the strong influence of peers, who are usually fools as well, students learn to despise good and to embrace evil. Those in positions of authority are regarded with contempt and are often the objects of violence. Promiscuity abounds, drugs and alcohol are widely used, and profanity and obscenities are common. Why would Christian parents want to place their children in this kind of environment *twelve years or more?*

## DESPISERS OF GOD'S WORD
### Proverbs 13:13

Ask yourself, "Is my child going to be placed in an environment that is conducive to the reading of Gods Word and one that promotes and teaches God's Word as divine?" If not, your child is in an institution that is under divine judgment.

*"Whoso despiseth the word shall be destroyed, but he that feareth the commandment shall be rewarded" (Proverbs 13:13).*

In June 1995, William B. was inspired to make his graduation from West High School in Salt Lake City, Utah, a memorable occasion. Little did he know just how memorable his graduation was going to be. William, in conjunction with the school's a cappella choir, was attempting to sing two songs which contained the words *Lord* and *God*.

Another student, Rachel B., and her parents, protested the religious overtones of the graduation ceremony. The issue was taken to court, and the Tenth Circuit Court of Appeals issued a restraining order against William and the others who were responsible for the religious elements of the graduation.

The plaintiffs felt the thrill of victory. Not willing to surrender so easily, however, William boldly went up on stage during the ceremony and invited his classmates to sing a final song called "Friends," written by Christian musician, Michael W. Smith. When the song began, school officials bodily dragged William off the stage—to the consternation of the majority of the parents and friends present.

Why were William and the other students reprimanded when they only wanted to sing a song with moral values as a "thank you" to the Lord for their friends and some teachers? Because the very nature of America's schools has fostered a hatred of God and of anything that resembles Christianity.

Shortly after I became a Christian in 1972, I began working as the noon director on a government elementary school campus in Culver City, California. My responsibility was to give guidance to the children during their playtime. Naturally, with children seven to twelve years of age, self-control is a learning process. I spent several months teaching the children how to play in harmony with each other. After breaking up fights, I would sit the children down together and share Biblical principles of being *"kind one to another, tenderhearted, forgiving one another, even as God for Christ's sake hath forgiven you" (Ephesians 4:32).*

I shared the love of Christ whenever possible. Within a year, the school grounds became a haven of joy and delight. The following school year, eager to return to school and resume my duties, I found the students equally joyful at my return and the campus in a peaceful state. The children would flock around me like bees to honey to hear stories from the Bible. Many children prayed to receive Christ as Savior.

All went well until these innocent children—some of whom were from another religious background—told their parents that they had received Christ during the noon hour at school. You can imagine how this went over—like a lead balloon. Needless to say, I was terminated, despite the fact that I was told that the campus had become as peaceful as any of the teachers could remember.

Why was I terminated? Because the school system, then and now, was and is opposed to the love of Christ. The system despises God's ways and His Word. Can you imagine the schools having this attitude back in the eighteenth and nineteenth centuries? Christians today boycott department stores over environmental or pro-life issues, but why will they not boycott government schools? Christian parents, I implore you to consider that government schools do not deserve your support!

## GREAT, WISE MEN AND WOMEN
### Proverbs 13:20

The Bible admonishes us to be under the influence of wise people, and this includes wise educators. The Bible further warns us not to be under the influence of fools.

*"He that walketh with wise men shall be wise, but a companion of fools shall be destroyed" (Proverbs 13:20).*

Parents, are your children surrounded with wise, Godly teachers and fellow students? If not, they may likely be destroyed in only a very short time in this environment which is hostile to Biblical principles and filled with improper role models.

I trust that most parents are familiar with America's history and its past Godly leaders who are now so often regarded with disdain. George Washington in many cases receives less respect, attention, and "textbook space" than Marilyn Monroe. Christopher Columbus is called an "Indian killer." U.S. History is taught from a non-providential perspective, and all acts of God, prayer by the Founding Fathers, and references to God directing the affairs of this nation have been removed from textbooks.

How do parents expect their children to rise to ever-higher levels of ability and to have goals of becoming great men and women when the government schools have removed or destroyed almost everything of lasting value in their histories and biographies? Children are being taught to walk with fools—not the wise.

We are commanded by God to teach only what is good and noble. We do not need schools that emphasize the faults of historical people and glorify those about whom we should be ashamed—a prevailing trend in today's history books. It is obvious that *"all have sinned and come short of the glory of God" (Romans 3:23).* We need to teach children that which is of value and that which is good in the lives of historical figures.

*"Finally, brethren, whatsoever things are true, whatsoever things are honest, whatsoever things are just, whatsoever things are pure, whatsoever things are lovely, whatsoever things are of good report; if there be any virtue, and if there be any praise, think on these things. Those things which ye have both learned, and received, and heard, and seen in me, do, and the God of peace shall be with you" (Philippians 4:8-9).*

Are your children in a school that is fulfilling Philippians 4:8-9? Are they learning to become great men and women of God? Are they walking *with* the wise and learning *of* the wise?

## RESCUE YOUR CHILDREN
### Psalm 144:11-12

King David cried out in a Messianic prophecy which echoes the cry of Christ among sinners. It can also apply to children crying out to parents to rescue them from the hands of sinners. A good point to keep in mind before reading the next Scripture is that if it were natural for children to leave parents and be indoctrinated in government schools at an early age, why do the majority of children at the age of five or so cry when taken to the bus stop or dropped off at school, "Mommy, please don't send me to school; I don't want to leave you; I'm scared!" Mom's cold reply is, "Grow up! It's not that bad. All children your age go to school. The end of the day will be here before you know it."

The Bible warns parents, *"Rid me, and deliver me from the hand of strange children, whose mouth speaketh vanity, and their right hand is a right hand of falsehood: That our sons may be as plants grown up in their youth; that our daughters may be as cornerstones, polished after the similitude of a palace"* (Psalm 144:11-12).

Do you wonder why America is not producing tender, precious, innocent, pure, and holy youth fit to adorn the palace of God? Consider where they spend their days.

Many educators do not send their own children to the current government schools. Even many of our government officials, who favor more and more government education financing, send their children to private schools. The maxim for a corrupt government is "do as I say, not as I do." Hypocrites! Parents, deliver your children now!

## THE WRATH OF GOD REVEALED
### Romans 1:18

*"For the wrath of God is revealed from heaven against all ungodliness and unrighteousness of men, who hold the truth in unrighteousness" (Romans 1:18).*

In this passage we can see that the Bible warns us about God's idea of those who hold truth in unrighteousness. They receive the "wrath of God." In government public schools today they teach evolution and godless science as truth—not theory. The danger lies in the fact that those who teach such lies will receive God's divine displeasure. When the judgment of God falls, it is not safe to be around. Why expose your children to an institution that will incur the divine judgment of God? The tragedy with Lot of old is that he became so accustomed to living among sinners, that he could not recognize impending judgment.

*"And when the morning arose, then the angels hastened Lot, saying, Arise, take thy wife, and thy two daughters, which are here; lest thou be consumed in the iniquity of the city. And while he lingered, the men laid hold upon his hand, and upon the hand of his wife, and upon the hand of his two daughters; the LORD being merciful unto him: and they brought him forth, and set him without the city" (Genesis 19:15-16).*

When fire and brimstone fell on Sodom, it would not have been safe to remain within the city limits. Can you imagine Lot telling the angels to wait until his girls came home from school before leaving the city of Sodom? Or that he needed a school transfer to move to the city of Zoar to re-enroll them in the Sodom Unified School System? Yet this is exactly what

20

Christian parents do when moving from place to place. The only difference is that they do not recognize the hand of God's judgment on the government schools of America today.

## COME OUT FROM THE UNCLEAN THING
### II Corinthians 6:14-18

*"Be ye not unequally yoked together with unbelievers: for what fellowship hath righteousness with unrighteousness? And what communion hath light with darkness? And what concord hath Christ with Belial? Or what part hath he that believeth with an infidel? And what agreement hath the temple of God with idols? For ye are the temple of the living God; as God hath said, I will dwell in them, and walk in them; and I will be their God, and they shall be my people. Wherefore come out from among them, and be ye separate, saith the Lord, and touch not the unclean thing; and I will receive you, And will be a Father unto you, and ye shall be my sons and daughters, saith the Lord Almighty" (II Corinthians 6:14-18).*

Most Christians apply this passage as a warning to their sons and daughters not to marry unbelievers. Businessmen apply it to becoming business partners with Christians instead of unbelievers. These are proper applications; yet, why do most parents not see that the warning applies to all areas of life—including sending their children to a school system that is not equally yoked with Christianity?

The Bible makes it clear that we should come out from among those who attempt to destroy our faith. The American school system, as it currently stands, is established for the purpose of destroying faith in the God Who created the world and in His Son Who died for the world.

The Bible also says that Christians are the temples of the Holy Ghost, and as such, we need to remain sanctified—set apart to hear and receive instruction that is pleasing to the Lord living within us. The conversations in classrooms and lunchrooms, more often than not, grieve the Holy Spirit living within us.

*"What! know ye not that your body is the temple of the Holy Ghost which is in you, which ye have of God, and ye are not your own? For ye are bought with a price; therefore, glorify God in your body and in your spirit, which are God's" (I Corinthians 6:19-20).*

*"And grieve not the Holy Spirit of God, whereby ye are sealed unto the day of redemption" (Ephesians 4:30).*

## DISCERNING GOOD FROM EVIL
### Hebrews 5:14

*"But strong meat belongeth to them that are of full age, even those who by reason of use have their senses exercised to discern both good and evil" (Hebrews 5:14).*

Do the public school systems in America teach discernment of good from evil? The obvious answer is "No!" In reality, they teach how to have "safe sex" by using condoms and birth control. That is not discernment, for the Bible warns that those who practice fornication, whether erroneously "safe" or not, will be thrown into the lake of fire.

*"But the fearful, and unbelieving, and the abominable, and murderers, and whoremongers [sexually immoral], and sorcerers [drug users], and idolaters, and all liars, shall have their part in the lake which burneth with fire and brimstone: which is the second death" (Revelation 21:8).*

Children kept in the public schools lose the ability to discern good from evil, because the schools teach that there are no absolutes, that parents are not always right, and that there may *not* be a God Who judges right from wrong. The American

22

schools have become like the nation of Israel of old, as the Prophet Isaiah warned:

*"Woe unto them that call evil good, and good evil; that put darkness for light, and light for darkness; that put bitter for sweet, and sweet for bitter!" (Isaiah 5:20).*

## THE FEAR OF THE LORD
### Proverbs 9:10

The Bible tells us that a good education consists of teaching the fear of the Lord.

*"The fear of the LORD is the beginning of wisdom, and the knowledge of the Holy is understanding" (Proverbs 9:10).*

*"The fear of the LORD is the beginning of wisdom. A good understanding have all they that do his commandments; his praise endureth for ever" (Psalm 111:10).*

In the national Standard Achievement Tests, scores are declining year after year. Rest assured, the schools are not teaching the fear of the Lord. Without being taught the fear of the Lord, children will never gain proper God-given wisdom. The books of Psalms and Proverbs are full of admonitions to parents and others to instruct children in wisdom. Government schools are not teaching wisdom; therefore, students are being trained to be self-centered and godless.

Government schools willfully neglect teaching the fear of the Lord and true wisdom because they do not believe in the Lord, nor the eternal punishment visited upon those who disregard Christ and God's divine mercy on sinners.

Within my lifetime I have witnessed a generation of students being trained to become atheistic and fearless of judgment for sin. The thought that American schools are producing reprobates and a godless, perverted generation that will rise up and root out Christ and the Christian principles that helped make America the greatest nation upon the earth is disheartening!

The Bible implies that sinners will continue to sin because there is no fear of God in their lives. *"The transgression of the wicked saith within my heart, that there is no fear of God before his eyes" (Psalm 36:1).*

To prove this, observe the government schools across America. It is not uncommon for some schools to be engaged in a losing battle of trying to control the use of guns, knives, sex, violence, profanity, drug use, alcohol addiction, lying, stealing, and disrespect of teachers and administrators among students.

Ask yourself, "Are schools better today than they were twenty years ago? Is there *more* fear of God and respect for His Word in the schools today—or *less*?" The answers to these questions will tell parents that public schools are not fit for the public—let alone Christian children. The Bible clearly tells us that a good education consists of teaching the fear of the Lord.

## TRAIN UP A CHILD
### Proverbs 22:6

The Bible makes it clear that parents are to train up their children.

*Proverbs 22:6* states, *"Train up a child in the way he should go; and when he is old, he will not depart from it."*

Seriously ask yourself whether the public school teachers and staff are going to care as much about your children's upbringing as you. Do they love them as much as you do? Will they use the rod of correction as God commands on sinful, self-willed, rebellious children who need training?

*"He that spareth his rod hateth his son; but he that loveth him chasteneth him betimes" (Proverbs 13:24).*

The modern American public school today has removed the "board of education" FROM rather than applying it TO "the seat of knowledge," as was practiced in the early American schools. As mentioned earlier, I received corporal punishment throughout my school years, my last swat coming in the eighth grade at John Adams Jr. High School in Santa Monica, California. Although not appreciated at the time, those instances of correction helped me become more civil.

One major cause of the moral waywardness of our children is that the government schools have departed from a Christian-based education and the proper discipline that alone can change the hearts of children by *"training them in the way they should go."* Instead, the schools have been training them in the way they *should not go.* Look around you. Do you see children lining the halls of public schools who are kind, genteel, obedient, respectful of their elders? Are their countenances full of innocence and joy? My experience has been the opposite.

Judgment is going to fall not only upon the government of this land, but also upon the parents who have allowed these corrupting influences to run unabated in our society.

*Hosea 4:1-7* states the following: *"Hear the word of the LORD, ye children of Israel: for the LORD hath a controversy with the inhabitants of the land, because there is no truth, nor mercy, nor knowledge of God in the land. By swearing, and lying, and killing, and stealing, and committing adultery, they break out, and blood toucheth blood.* [Sounds like government schools in local neighborhoods throughout our nation.] *Therefore shall the land mourn, and everyone that dwelleth therein shall languish, with the beasts of the field, and with the fowls of heaven; yea, the fishes of the sea also shall be taken away. Yet let no man strive, nor reprove another: for thy people are as they that strive with the priest. Therefore shalt thou fall in the day, and the prophet also shall fall with thee in the night, and I will destroy thy mother.* [Parents will receive judgment of the Lord.] *My people are destroyed for lack of knowledge: because thou hast rejected knowledge,* **I will also reject thee, that thou shalt be no priest to me: seeing thou hast forgotten the law of thy God, I will also forget thy children. As they were increased, so they sinned against me: therefore will I change their glory into shame.*"*

If you want to see where a nation is heading, take a close look at the youth it is producing. God judges a nation by the shame of its youth. Far too many of America's youth are shameful in clothing styles, hairstyles, attitudes, and the marking of tattoos and earrings they wear all over their bodies. The above text from Hosea lays the judgment of a nation on the priests and parents of the land. Biblically speaking, Christian parents are kings and priests in their respective families. As priests, they are responsible before God to train their children. As a home-school parent, I often discipline my children in a multitude of ways to produce Godly, Christlike character. However, if my children were in a public school, I know full well the officials would not be nearly as committed to their character development as I am. Even if a public school teacher had great intentions of helping students develop character, there are neither the disciplinary resources available nor the time to do a thorough job in light of all the other students and responsibilities a teacher has.

A possible response to my arguments might be, "You may have described unbelievers' children, but not *my* children who attend the public school system. They are wonderfully well-behaved children." I applaud you if your children are remaining sweet, tender, and loving to you as parents, and hungry for the things of God and His Word. If that is the case, why are you sending your lambs to be educated among wolves? The prophet Ezekiel lays a great judgment upon the prophets and priests of a nation. Those priests and prophets who lead by bad example receive judgment. The role of a prophet and priest is to lead the people of God in the ways of the Lord. By setting a bad example and not teaching right from wrong, the priests and prophets lead the flock of God to the paths of destruction.

Ezekiel 22:25-30: *"There is a conspiracy of her prophets in the midst thereof, like a roaring lion ravening the prey; they have devoured souls. Her priests have violated my law, and have profaned mine holy things: they have put no difference between the holy and profane, neither have they shewed difference between the unclean and the clean. And I sought for a man among them, that should make up the hedge, and stand in the gap before me for the land, that I should not destroy it: but I found none."*

I believe the Lord is looking for parents, pastors and church leaders in America today to stand up for principles and pull their children out of godless, Christ-hating, socialistic, sexually perverted, unpatriotic government schools across this land. Those pastors and parents who accept and condone the government schools in America today will have morally and spiritually bankrupt children as the consequence of their choice. As an evangelist who has traveled through 48 states, I know countless pastors and church leaders whose children have become sexually promiscuous and carnal in their life goals and aspirations. The godless schools of this land have helped destroy church leaders' children right under their noses. Church leaders also need to question why they are sending their children to godless institutions of higher learning. Perhaps it is because of the peer pressure that other government school devotees place upon them. Have the church leaders of this land become fearful of men instead of God? Have they become like Aaron—bowing down before the golden calf and pressured into idolatry by a rebellious people?

## SPORTS PROGRAMS
### I Timothy 4:7-8

Many Christian parents have told me that they placed their child in a government school, knowing it was not the best choice, simply because it had a great sports program. They claimed that since their child loves sports and finds fulfillment in them, they were doing what was best for the individual "needs" of the child. In answer to this excuse I often quote I Timothy 4:7-8: *"And exercise thyself rather unto godliness. For bodily exercise profiteth little: but godliness is profitable unto all things, having promise of the life that now is, and of that which is to come."* Jesus told us to *"Seek ye first the kingdom of God" (Matthew 6:33),* not basketball or football.

Frankly, parents and church leaders would have to admit that America has made an idol of sports and entertainment. One cannot deny this in light of the tremendous salaries of professional athletes and entertainment celebrities. Where are our nation's values when athletes and entertainers receive far more money than do Godly teachers dedicated to train students to become moral, productive citizens? What does it say about our culture when entertainers receive more than medical doctors?

To place a child in a government school for sports is a poor and short-sighted decision. When I served on a school board several years ago, another Christian man and I suggested that high school students not be permitted to participate in sports for the school unless they had at least a "C" average in all their subjects. After the vote was approved and the policy implemented, some parents cried, "Unfair!" because their children were not getting C's. These parents contended that denying their children a chance at competitive sports would damage their self-esteem. Even more disturbing to me was that many of these complaining parents were from the church where I was youth pastor at the time. Jesus said, *"Where your treasure is, there will your heart be also" (Matthew 6:21).*

Furthermore, organized competitive sports, especially in a public school, can be spiritually dangerous to the Christian, for two reasons.

First, if a student excels in a sport, the popularity without the mature fruit of humility accompanying stardom can produce a spirit of pride. Admiration by other students can influence the Christian student to be silent about his or her faith, for fear of rejection and loss of popularity. For the boys, sports involvement usually causes girls to notice and pursue them, which can lead to immorality. The world's strongest man, Samson, was destroyed by a foolish weakness in his *character.*

Second, if the student does not excel in competitive sports, he or she tries all the harder to derive self-esteem from peers, which will lead down the road to ruin. Seeking the praise of man over the glory of God will *always* bring problems.

Many government-school sports players that I have known throughout my life have had temptations along with their sports. For the boys, the temptations were of the "wine, women, and song" variety. The "party animal" is usually closely intertwined with the school sports scene, and in this arena, the temptations are too great for the young Christian. During the teen years it is difficult to pursue God and the disciplines of a Godly Christian life while developing a competitive edge. This is why the Apostle Paul said, *"Bodily exercise profiteth little."*

Are parents sending signals to their children that sports is the ultimate fulfillment in life? Have sports become a "sacred cow" to many well-meaning Christians?

All this is not to say, however, that physical exercise is wrong. Not at all. We are to be good stewards of our physical bodies, and this concept would include maintaining physical fitness. There are many opportunities for *family* sports activities, and certainly, much work around the house, garden, and farm involves physical work—and some of it, hard work.

Children and teens can be taught to serve widows: cleaning, gardening, mowing the lawn, chopping wood, shoveling snow, trimming trees, etc. Churches, retreat centers, and Christian camps are always in need of volunteers for manual labor.

Older teens may want to consider starting a local moving business. People are always looking for reliable, responsible, low-cost moving help. Other home businesses available to teens would be yard/garden work, window-washing, heavy house cleaning, and much more, all of which would build physical strength and fitness—but for Godly purposes.

## WHERE ARE YOUR CHILDREN ROOTED?
### Colossians 2:6-8

The Bible tells us that after becoming Christians we are to become *"rooted in Christ" (Colossians 2:6-8).* We are warned to beware of *"vain philosophy"* and improper *"rudiments of the world"* that teach ANTICHRIST doctrine. Schools capitalize on vain godless philosophy; therefore, placing a child in the system as it now stands is in direct disobedience to God and his Word.

*"As ye have therefore received Christ Jesus the Lord, so walk ye in him: Rooted and built up in him, and established in the faith, as ye have been taught, abounding therein with thanksgiving. Beware lest any man spoil you through*

*philosophy and vain deceit, after the tradition of men, after the rudiments of the world, and not after Christ" (Colossians 2:6-8).*

It is helpful to break down the amount of time into hours per year children are being subjected to negative influences in the public school. Let's assume a school day starting around 7:55 A.M. and dismissing at 2:55 P.M. Taking into account that they have one 20-minute recess period and a 30-minute lunch period, it can be assumed that they receive about 6 hours of instruction per day. Now multiply that by the number of scheduled school days (177 days) in the school year, to total 1062 hours of classroom instruction yearly. In twelve years of public school education, a child will have received 12,744 hours of humanistic instruction.

The defense parents often make is, "I teach them the Bible, and they go to church and receive Bible training." Let us look at the facts of this self-deceptive thought. If your child is in school and away from home 7 hours a day, you have the opportunity for parental guidance from about 3:30 P.M. to 9:30 P.M. Realistically, how many of those 6 hours that your child is home and awake do you spend debriefing him or her and giving Bible study? For argument's sake, let's assume that you are extremely disciplined and diligent to do daily study and fulfill the above admonition in Colossians of *rooting and grounding your children in Christ.*

By spending 1 hour a night, 4 nights a week, in focused Bible study, 4 hours of study will have occurred by Friday. Taking into account church time, there is a possibility of 1 hour at a midweek service, 2 hours Sunday morning and 1 hour Sunday night. With the combination of home and church, your child could amass a total of 8 hours of Christian study and fellowship weekly. Assuming that you maintain this schedule every single week for 52 weeks in a year, your child will have received 416 hours of Biblical instruction for the year. Compared with the 1062 hours of humanistic instruction in a year, the 416 hours of Christian instruction seems rather paltry. Remember the figure of 416 hours represents the rather unrealistic assumption that families would have the discipline to maintain this demanding schedule without fail.

In reality, the average family lifestyle is so fast paced that unless there is a commitment to its importance very little time is spent in dedicated instruction of children. The schools have plenty of time to give to your children since, after all, they are hired by you through property taxes to do this demanding job every day (however poorly they do it).

American parents have been brainwashed to believe that "professionals" should do most of the instruction of their children. Why have they allowed themselves to persist in the deception that public schools are far superior to what they could offer their children themselves? A major reason, if forced to admit it, is that many parents make the excuse they are too busy to spend the necessary time teaching their children. Parents have become selfish with their time. They also feel, although they may not admit it, that their children are too difficult to deal with. They would rather let "professionals" deal with the behavior of their children. In God's eyes, the title "professional" does not qualify someone to instruct or teach. If the "professionals" are godless, they cannot be Biblically qualified.

## SALT AND LIGHT
### Matthew 5:13-16

Jesus said in Matthew 5:13-16: *"Ye are the salt of the earth: but if the salt have lost its savour, wherewith shall it be salted? It is thenceforth good for nothing, but to be cast out and trodden under foot of men. Ye are the light of the world. A city that is set on a hill cannot be hid. Neither do men light a candle, and put it under a bushel, but on a candlestick; and it givith light unto all that are in the house. Let your light so shine before men that may see your good works, and glorify your Father in heaven."*

Far too many Christian parents use the above Scripture to justify placing their children in a local government school, saying that their children are commissioned to be *"salt and light"* on the school campus. Or that they lead Bible studies and prayer meetings, that they meet with other Christian youth once a year at the flag pole. For years, Christian parents have told me that they place their tender children in public schools so their children will evangelize other lost youth and teachers.

I would like to challenge this weak use of Scripture. Obviously, Christ has commissioned believers to *"Go ye therefore, and teach all nations, baptizing them in the name of the Father, and of the Son, and of the Holy Ghost: Teaching them to observe all things whatsoever I have commanded you: and, lo, I am with you alway, even unto the end of the world"* (Matthew 28:19-20). However, in Luke 24:49, Jesus commands the disciples to *"tarry ye in the city of Jerusalem, until ye be endued with power from on high."* Mind you, he is speaking to adults to tarry. It stands to reason that if Christ admonished his own adult disciples, who were with Him night and day for three years, not to go out and evangelize until they received *"power from on high,"* how then is it that parents can send their young inexperienced children to convert the campus? Christ sent out His *adult* disciples two by two, knowing the dangers and pressures they would face in a hostile environment. In the New Testament, a person studying the texts will never find reference to Christ sending youth out to change the world and evangelize the lost. Believe me, youth between five and eighteen *are* the mission field. They themselves need to be discipled and built up with the power of God's Word. Even after David the shepherd boy killed Goliath, he returned to shepherding, not a public ministry.

Apart from a very small percentage of cases, the grim reality is that Christian youth are influenced by the unsaved youth and their subculture. I speak from experience, having worked with youth in government schools for more than 24 years. Just look at the facts. Normally it is not the Christian students who are doing the most to promote Christian values among unsaved students; rather, it is the unsaved youth who are doing the most to destroy the morals of the Christian students. Christian boys did not learn to wear earrings from hanging around Godly Christian boys in a Christian church or home school. The weird hairstyles did not come from the Christian home. The taste for wild music and godless movie viewing did not come from Godly parents or pastors. The haughty rebellious "bad attitude" toward adult authority did not come from a Godly environment. It came from the godless government school system. As a former youth pastor, I recall visiting our church youth at the local high school campus on various occasions. Several were actually embarrassed at my presence. After all, what would their peers think if they were seen with a pastor?

For years I have heard Christian parents tell me that their children are going to make the difference in the local school systems, yet how many schools do you know of that are changing their curriculum for a more moral and Godly one because Christian youth have "evangelized" the schools? How many schools have sought to improve their baccalaureates, making them more Christ-centered because of the influence of the Christian youth in the school? How many have cut out pagan Halloween festivities because of the Christian influence? How many schools have returned to the celebration of Hanukkah, and a Christ-centered Christmas? How many schools are reinstating the Ten Commandments on the school walls? How many schools are teaching the youth to pray for their teachers and their nation like the Christian students at the flag pole? The answer is *none*. Why? Jesus tells us why. *"If you are not for me, you are against me" (Matthew 12:30)*. Wake up! Children should not be in a system opposed to Christ and the Gospel. The current schools are openly hostile to Christ, but tolerant of all other world religions.

If every evangelical Christian family in America that had their children in the state schools across the land decided to protest and say, "Enough is enough!" and seek private Christian or home school education, then the government would be faced with one of two choices: Either force parents by law to enroll their children in the government school (God forbid we succumb to that someday!), or repent and apologize to parents for the lack of foresight on their part, and invite Christians to have complete control of the public schools, as in the early days of our nation. Your cry is, "That would be impossible!" I heartily agree with you. The system has become so intolerant toward Christianity that the Lord must write *Ichabod* on its doors.*

If Christ Himself applied for a teaching position, He would be denied under the false understanding of the "Church-and State-separation issue." Please do not try to defend the godless government school system. There are no Biblical positions to stand on. *"Do not cast your pearls [precious children] before swine to be trampled under foot" (Matthew 7:6)*.

* *Ichabod* means "The glory is departed." ( See I Samuel 4:21.)

## COMBAT ZONE
### Ephesians 4:32-5:7

*"And be ye kind one to another, tenderhearted, forgiving one another, even as God for Christ's sake hath forgiven you. Be ye therefore followers of God, as dear children; And walk in love, as Christ also hath loved us, and hath given himself for us an offering and a sacrifice to God for a sweetsmelling savour. But fornication, and all uncleanness, or covetousness, let it not be once named among you, as becometh saints; Neither filthiness, nor foolish talking, nor jesting, which are not convenient: but rather giving of thanks. Let no man deceive you with vain words: for because of these things cometh the wrath of God upon the children of disobedience. Be not ye therefore partakers with them" (Ephesians 4:32-5:7).*

What would you think of parents who allowed their children, while vacationing at the beach, to swim in shark-infested waters? What if you approached the parents to warn them of the dangers, and pointed out to them that those fins are man-eating sharks, and they retorted, "Oh, it's not that bad. Besides, my child is going to have to face sharks someday, so it may as well be now."

This example is not too far from the truth of the conditions in the current government schools in America. Parents are blindly placing their children in "shark-infested" schools.

The other day, while doing some shopping, I ran into a Christian friend from our local church. After small talk, the home-school mother told me she had placed her thirteen-year-old daughter into the "good local neighborhood junior high," because the girl was "scared of public school kids," and she wanted to help her daughter overcome the fear. The mother then proceeded to tell me that within two weeks, the daughter was accosted by three lesbian classmates who wanted to include her as a lover.

The mother brought it to the attention of the principal when the girls were persistent in pursuing the daughter. Additional false accusations spread that her tender, innocent daughter had had an affair with a faculty member. As I walked away, I was *grieved* that the mother still felt that the public school was the best place for her daughter. What will it take for parents to wake up?

I do not know about your junior high school years. Perhaps you went to a nice junior high school, so to speak. Well, I certainly did not. I spent the entire three years fighting for my rights to my lunch and well-being. Today I suffer the ill effects of a broken nose from fist fighting my way through those three years. It was in junior high that I was introduced to pornography, profanity, drugs, and sex. Why would parents in their right minds want to expose their child to such corruption at such an early age, in light of Ephesians 4:32-5:7?

You may say that it is not that bad in the particular school in which you plan to place your children. My challenge to parents is to go to the school for a few days, with spiritual eyes open, and observe the attitude of the students and teachers. I believe that you will change your mind after that experience.

The Biblical goal of parents should be to keep their children tender and innocent to evil, and prepared for the Lord. The government schools in some communities are so dangerous that many schools throughout the land where Christian children attend have to have metal detectors to help confiscate dangerous weapons. The local public school is certainly not a place for right-minded Christian parents to place their beloved children unless they do not care that they become tough and hardened in order to survive.

I found a good test to see how tender children are toward their parents. Walk around the campus and hold your teen's hand, or kiss him or her on the cheek as he or she is dropped off for school. I have found that the majority of Christian youth will shun the parent in embarrassment.

Our pre-teen son, and our teen and young adult daughters welcome our attention and associate with peers and adults alike. They are not embarrassed to be around us, and are not pressured to think like most peer-oriented youth that parents are "nerds." Could you imagine Christ being embarrassed of Mary and Joseph at the age of twelve when they found Him in the Temple among the Jewish leaders?

What makes tender children into hardened rebels is the constant barrage of godless peer conformity. It is "survival of the fittest." Look at the "infested waters" of current government schools' combat zones:

1. One in five American high school students regularly smoke marijuana. Fifteen percent of teenagers have tried cocaine.
2. Teenage sex has produced 250,000 illegitimate births annually and countless abortions. There is an epidemic of venereal disease. Six out of ten 16 to 18-year-olds say they have had sexual intercourse. In the 13 to 15-year age group, the number is 1 out of 3.
3. Suicide is the second-leading cause of death among teenagers. Of the young people who committed suicide in 1996, 4,000 were 15-19 years of age, and 550 were 14 or under.
4. In one major, well-known city, 19% of the teaching staff of 3,000 live in fear of student attacks. Ten percent of the teachers have been attacked, and this fear shapes

their reluctance to deal with problems that arise in the classroom.

One Christian high school teacher of a supposedly small community "safe" school district told me on various occasions she witnessed teens necking in class and engaging in other deeds too vile to mention here. She said she would not report them for fear she would lose her job, or be assaulted by the students. Teachers have reported that 40% of the students have been assaulted by other students. Is it any wonder that the many government school teachers do not have their own children in a government school?

Parents may respond, "My school district is not that bad, because we live in a small community." Parents, I pastored in a small community, and no community is spared moral decadence.

## WHERE IS YOUR CHILD "SITTING"?
### Psalm 1:1-6

The Bible makes it very clear where we are *not* to sit and receive instruction. I believe parents are aware that the government of America has allowed social architects to alter the public schools from their Christ-centered foundation in early America. These social changers have an agenda to make the government schools into secular humanistic institutions, where man is honored—not God.

This may sound far-fetched, but consider this quote from *The Humanist Magazine*, a magazine subscribed to by a multitude of educators:

*"I am convinced that the battle for humankind's future must be won in the public school classroom by teachers who*

*correctly perceive their role as the proselytizers of a new faith: a religion of humanity that recognizes and respects what theologians call divinity in every human being. These teachers must embody the same selfless dedication as the most rabid fundamentalist preachers, for they will be ministers of another sort, utilizing a classroom instead of a pulpit to convey humanist values in whatever subject they teach, regardless of the educational level—preschool day care center or large state university. The classroom must and will become an arena of conflict between the old and the new—the rotting corpse of Christianity, together with all its adjacent evils and misery, and the new faith of humanism. . . It will undoubtedly be a long, arduous, painful struggle, replete with much sorrow and many tears, but humanism will emerge triumphant. It must if the family of humankind is to survive."* The Humanist Magazine, January/February 1983, p.26.

Read the following passage in the Bible and ask yourself if your child should be sitting under the instruction of a godless system of government education. The first Psalm is so familiar that often one does not consider its ramifications and applications to daily life. It only becomes a psalm we memorize because it sounds so good. The danger with Christians is that we can often read the Scripture and become, as the Apostle James warns in James 1:22-23: "A hearer of the word and not a doer of the word."

Psalm 1:1-6 sounds a warning: *"Blessed is the man that walketh not in the counsel of the ungodly, nor standeth in the way of sinners, nor sitteth in the seat of the scornful. But his delight is in the law of the LORD; and in his law doth he meditate day and night. And he shall be like a tree planted by the rivers of water, that bringeth forth his fruit in his season; his leaf also shall not wither; and whatsoever he doeth shall prosper. The ungodly are not so: but are like the chaff which the wind driveth away. Therefore the ungodly shall not stand in the judgment, nor sinners in the congregation of the righteous. For the LORD knoweth the way of the righteous: but the way of the ungodly shall perish."* (See also Psalm 26.)

## THE UNIVERSITIES OF THIS LAND
### Proverbs 3:5-6

Even the secular universities of this land are, by and large, politically and morally corrupt. Sending a child to receive an education in a system and giving thousands of dollars to a system that is helping to destroy our nation does not make sense. I believe that only in rare cases have leaders and parents truly heard from the Lord that they should send their children to a secular college or university—and only after serious prayer and fasting. Do not be deceived into thinking that just because the student is receiving a scholarship and the school is being paid for by others, that this is the will of God for your child. Even Satan offered Jesus the world if He would surrender His Lordship to Satan. Other options are available, and the Lord will lead those who seek Him as to the future of their *(His)* children. The "sacred cow" of godless education is not always God's will. Yes, He can lead a young person there and make what is "meant for evil, good." The important thing is this: Do not send a young person to a school of higher learning unless you have heard from *the higher power—God.* My life verse applies here: *"Trust in the LORD with all thine heart; and lean not unto thine own understanding. In all thy ways acknowledge him, and he shall direct thy paths" (Proverbs 3:5-6).*

Since you have read this far, and you perceive how radical and extreme I appear, I may well drive in one more "nail" before making my closing statements. My wife, Marilyn, and I have had to cross this higher learning "bridge," since at the time of writing this guide, we have a 20-year-old daughter. After spending time in prayer and Bible study, we have adopted a position that seems extreme in light of America's current trend.

Biblically speaking, you cannot find that God places responsibilities upon women other than as a wife supporting her husband by being a helpmeet and raising Godly children. I do not intend to imply that a woman is to be intellectually suppressed, but rather propose that there are alternatives in preparing young women for their elevated role as wives and mothers or single women of Godly character. Have you investigated the Spirit-led alternatives, or are you simply pursuing the traditions of men by enrolling your daughters in heathen universities which have no regard for their spiritual instruction?

Think this through. The young collegiate woman graduates after years of study and having spent a small fortune. At best, she finds a well-paying job in the profession she pursued, meets *Mr. Perfect,* gets married, and within a year or two finds herself with a child, and is now faced with a dilemma. The God-given instinct is to be a stay-at-home mother, but their financial trap of relying on two incomes and a godless society pressure her to go back to work. After all, she is a "career woman." If she chooses to go to work and have the day-care center raise her child, society applauds her, but God is grieved. If she chooses to stay home and give up her profession to raise a Godly family, society frowns and says, "How wasteful! You spent your parents' life savings to receive a degree to prepare you for a professional career, only to find yourself choosing to raise your children at home." I would have to agree that the money was poorly spent. A better investment would have been to apply it toward a house and baby furniture, leaving the support of the family to the bread winner—the husband—to toil by the "sweat of his brow." The breakdown of our society is caused partially by "stay-away-from-home" mothers who think they will find fulfillment in the work world. All they will end up with is frustration and desiring a family at a time when perhaps it will be too late.

As for me and my house, we have chosen to keep our daughters home—protected, sheltered in love, and trained to become Godly, submissive wives someday. Lord willing, our greatest joy will be that their husbands will someday come up to us as parents and say, "Thank you for relying on Christ in raising the most wonderful, submissive wife I could have ever imagined. She is content to love me and find complete fulfillment in supporting me and being a Godly mother raising Godly children."

Again, I challenge parents to consider why are they sending their daughters from the home into secular universities. Alternatives may be private tutoring or correspondence courses that fulfill their desire to learn. To clarify a young woman's goal in continued education, she should ask herself, "Is what I am learning going to be a benefit to my relationship with God my father, and perhaps future husband and children?"

For the sons in a family, again, the general rule *"trust in the Lord"* applies. Prayer for direction is extremely important. Not all young men need to go to universities to become successful. Success comes from the Lord, *"For promotion cometh neither from the east, nor from the west, nor from the south" (Psalm 75:6).* In our next section I will address the issue of success and promotion.

## GAINING FAVOR WITH GOD AND MAN
### Luke 2:52

*"And Jesus increased in wisdom and stature, and in favour with God and man"(Luke 2:52).* What good is a profession and lots of success and money if you have not "gained favor with God?" If a person has not gained favor in the sight of God first, then he or she has missed life's fullest joy and purpose. The majority of universities, and unfortunately, some Bible schools, have missed the mark in their real purpose in training their students. Look at the early universities of America's past to see the purposes in their establishment. They were run and operated by committed, evangelical Christians who wanted to train students to serve Christ in all walks of life. The Bible was the major source of education, and the goal of professors was to train the students to reason Biblically. With a Bible training basis, a graduate could enter a profession and apply the principles of the Word of God in his other chosen field, therefore establishing and keeping America a Godly nation, full of Biblical principle and character. Look around at this sin-sick society, and you will see that the schools of "higher" learning have neglected their proper job of education.

William Henry Seward, Secretary of State under Lincoln, was also vice-president of the American Bible Society. He said:

*"I know not how long a republican government can flourish among a great people who have not the Bible; the experiment has never been tried; But this I do know: that the existing government of this country never could have had existence but for the Bible.*

*And, further, I do, in my conscience, believe that if at every decade of years a copy of the Bible could be found in every family in the land, its republican institutions would be perpetuated."*

America's "republican institutions" are on the verge of collapse because the educators of America's students have willfully neglected God and have lost God's favor. We have not only lost God's favor, but we have lost favor with man. The nations of the world once looked to America as their example. Today, America is viewed with disdain and hatred by many formerly loyal nations.

I believe Christ should be our example in all areas of life. In the area of education He serves as a wonderful example, as seen in Philippians 2:3-9:

*"Let nothing be done through strife or vainglory; but in lowliness of mind let each esteem other better than themselves. Look not every man on his own things, but every man also on the things of others. Let this mind be in you, which was also in Christ Jesus: Who, being in the form of God, thought it not robbery to be equal with God: **But made himself of no reputation**, and took upon him the form of a servant, and was made in the likeness of men: And being found in fashion as a man, he humbled himself, and became obedient unto death, even the death of the cross. Wherefore God also hath highly exalted him, and given him a name which is above every name."*

Christ, as God, humbled Himself and became a man. As a man, He humbled Himself and emptied Himself of His pre-existent "Godness." In Greek, this emptying is called *Kenosis,* which implies that Christ retained His divine nature, but limited Himself to human attributes and powers during the days of His flesh, so He could be a true example of a sinless human anointed with the Spirit to defeat Satan. His power and ability came completely by dependence upon God.

During the time of Christ, there were educational facilities. The Greeks, Romans, and Hebrews loved the quest of knowledge. As a human, Christ chose rather to depend upon the Spirit, not on an education, to be all the Father called Him to be. Prior to Christ's ascension He commissioned His followers to wait for the Holy Spirit before moving out to serve Him—not to go to school. The Bible says that the haters of Christ disdained the disciples as mere "ignorant fishermen." Would to God we had more such "ignorant fishermen" today!

With this in mind, should parents not wait for the same Holy Spirit to lead them to place their young adult children in higher fields of study? Could not the same Holy Spirit Who moved Christ, and later His followers who turned the "world upside down," not empower our children to be used where He leads them to impact the nation and world? Can parents not see that it is not the education we have or do not have that changes the world for God's glory, but it is the *Holy Spirit* in an individual yielded to the Lord who is going to make the difference in life! Parents must understand that education is not an end in itself—*Christ* is! As a parent, I would rather protect my children from schooling that is not led by the Spirit of God. Our goal as parents is not to produce educated children, but children who will "gain favor with God" first, and man second.

## WHAT'S A PARENT TO DO?
### Deuteronomy 6:1-7

*"Now these are the commandments, the statutes, and the judgments, which the LORD your God commanded to teach you, that ye might do them in the land whither ye go to possess it: That thou mightest fear the LORD thy God, to keep all his statutes and his commandments, which I command thee, thou, and thy son, and thy son's son, all the days of thy life; and that*

*thy days may be prolonged. Hear therefore, O Israel, and observe to do it; that it may be well with thee, and that ye may increase mightily, as the LORD God of thy fathers hath promised thee, in the land that floweth with milk and honey. Hear, O Israel: The LORD our God is one LORD: And thou shalt love the LORD thy God with all thine heart, and with all thy soul, and with all thy might. ◦ And these words, which I command thee this day, shall be in thine heart: And thou shalt teach them diligently unto thy children, and shalt talk of them when thou sittest in thine house, and when thou walkest by the way, and when thou liest down, and when thou risest up"* (Deuteronomy 6:1-7).

## THERE ARE TWO CHOICES:
### A. Church/Community Christian School

If both parents feel that they must work, or in the case of the single parent, there is the alternative of Christian school education. These parents can choose to delegate their God-given responsibility to Godly educators within the confines of a Christian school. I applaud the fact that Christian educators have sacrificed a higher standard of living by choosing to teach in a Christian school, as they earn a fraction of the salary that government teachers do.

I also wholeheartedly commend Christian educators who work within the government schools throughout the land. The mature, Godly Christian teacher has one of the greatest mission fields in the world right in a public school classroom. While I heartily approve of Christian teachers in the public schools, I believe it spells disaster to place your impressionable children in that same hostile environment.

Parents, it is important to realize that although your child may have a Christian teacher in a government school, the environment, textbooks, and other students exert a far greater influence on your child than does that teacher. If you allow your child to remain in that school, you would still be sacrificing him or her on the altar of humanism.

A word to the wise in choosing a Christian school: Just because the name on the building may be a Christian name, beware. Satan specializes in appearing as an angel of light:

*"And no marvel; for Satan himself is transformed into an angel of light" (II Corinthians 11:14).*

Use the following suggestions in evaluating and choosing a Godly Christian school:

1. Walk around the campus; watch how the students behave toward one another. Listen to how they talk to each other. Is their speech honoring to the Lord?

2. Sit in on several classes and observe how the teachers instruct the students entrusted to them and if the students are respectful to the teachers.

3. Look at as many textbooks as possible. Some Christian schools use government textbooks in major subjects such as history, science, and health.

4. What is the school environment like? (Posters, displays, etc.)

5. Attend at least three chapels to see the caliber of the spiritual climate the school is attempting to foster. Some Christian schools do not even have chapel.

6. What are the students' clothing styles like? Hairstyles? Jewelry? Make-up? Are the girls modest and distinctly feminine? Are the boys distinctly masculine?

7. Observe the lunch area. Remember, your child will learn from peers about movies, music, and fads. Are you prepared for this? In many of the 500 or so Christian schools that I have spoken in over the past 18 years, the

students, for all practical purposes, talked, behaved, and dressed, like government school students. The only things that could be called "Christian" were some of the teachers, the name on the building, and perhaps the textbooks, along with a handful of faithful students.

8. Watch the behavior of students in grades 5-12 in the area of boy-girl relationships. Do the students seem preoccupied with the opposite sex? Do they hold hands or even hang all over each other?

9. Investigate the sports program, if your child is inclined toward sports. What is the attitude of team players? I have seen Christian students and sometimes even coaches use profanity and display bad attitudes and poor sportsmanship. And many girl cheerleaders dress very immodestly.

You may be thinking that no school would have such high standards. I admit that these standards *are* high, but your children are worthy of high standards. Paul admonishes Christians to *"press toward the mark for the prize of the **high calling** of God in Christ Jesus" (Philippians 3:14).* I can assure you that there are many Godly Christian schools throughout the USA that *do* meet the above standards. I have ministered in them. There are also many Christian schools that fall tragically short of these standards.

I vividly recall ministering in a large, well-known Christian school in Southern California. I asked the principal if I was going to address mostly non-Christian students or Christian students. He assured me that the majority would be believers, and that in order to attend the school, at least one parent had to be a professing Christian. With this in mind, I chose my Scripture text and planned a powerful conclusion with an altar time of repentance and prayer. Of the 500 ninth-through twelfth-grade students, only two came forward.

One of the two, a twelfth-grade boy, told me that the students were mocking me and that they thought they were saved. His father was one of the pastors on staff at the church which sponsored this school. He told me that the majority of students got drunk on the weekends, had wild parties, and that the girls who appeared to be the most chaste were "all show," because on the weekends they were sexually involved.

This big, strong eighteen-year-old broke down and started sobbing. He told me that he was fooling his family and acting like a Christian, but living like the devil with all his school buddies. He had recently repented and found true salvation, and he now really cared for the other students and was concerned for their salvation. Make sure you investigate thoroughly what appears to be a Christian school.

## B. Christian Home Education

Having had two of our children in Christian schools for part of their elementary education, and now home educating all three, I can speak from experience on both sides. By far, the most challenging form of education is home education; however, as with most difficult undertakings, the results often prove to be the most rewarding. Anything worth attaining in life is difficult. Carrying a child for nine months and then going through labor and delivery is difficult for any woman, but who would negate the value of such work?

Home education is just an extension of the love that parents have for their children. Why go through five or six years of early training only to turn your children over to others to educate for the next twelve years? It just does not make sense to allow someone else—and in most cases, perfect strangers—to have such a tremendous influence on your children. Home education allows you to hand-pick the curricula your children need. It removes the unfair pressure on their young tender spirits that they are not as "smart" as the peers whom they look up to. It allows them to learn at their own speed and develop the God-given gifts and callings instilled in them at conception. Unencumbered by government school regulations, many home-educated students graduate from high school at age 15 or 16, and they can then move into the areas of life to which the Lord has called them.

After 14 years of speaking to thousands of home-educating parents in 48 states, I can honestly say that the fruit of home schooling is by far the most rewarding. The students are more wholesome, "innocent to that which is evil," intelligent, well-adjusted, and able to communicate in an adult fashion with adults, and in a loving fashion with younger children. What is more, they score higher on the Standard Achievement Tests.

Most parents feel incapable of teaching their children, and many do not want to have their children around all day. Sending their children to an outside school is a relief in some ways; yet, deep down, parents who send their children out for others to educate feel guilty. They know, whether or not they will admit it, that their children are *their* primary responsibility. On the day we stand before the Lord, we will not be able to say, "Lord it's not *my* fault my children turned out so badly; it's their *teachers'* fault."

Another reason parents will not educate their children at home is they feel that they must have two incomes to make ends meet. It has been proven that when a woman works outside the home and adds up all the extra expense of travel, clothing, insurance, taxes, child-care, lunches out, and fast-food dinners for the family, she brings home very little. I firmly believe that the Lord will reward parents who are committed to training their children at home. I even know of single parents who are so committed to raising Godly children that they home educate *and* hold down a full-time job.

**If you are interested in home education, there are several sources of help and information available to you:**
1. If you subscribe to an on-line service, look up the word *home school*, and you will find a multitude of message boards, websites, etc., that will help you.
2. Your church probably has some home-educating families. They can help steer you in the right direction.
3. **The Teaching Home** magazine has information on home-education leaders in your area who can help you:
   **The Teaching Home, P.O. Box 20219**
   **Portland, OR 97294**
   **(503) 253-9633**

## CONCLUSION:

I realize that this booklet is difficult for many readers to digest. All I ask is that you pray about it, with no preconceived notions. Ask the Lord to show you His will for your family in light of the Scripture passages you have read.

I recall the time that I went to an evangelistic meeting where the now-deceased Keith Green was ministering in music and the Word. I walked out because I felt that he was harsh, uncaring, and did not understand the grace of God. Two years later the Lord got hold of me and revealed areas in my sinful life that showed me that what Keith Green preached was exactly what I needed to hear. The problem was not with Keith Green—but with *me*.

Today, eighteen years later, I am harder on myself than Keith Green ever was. I have grown spiritually and have seen things differently. Change is good when the Lord is allowed to direct. May He direct your steps in this most vital area of life—the education of your precious children. Remember that no one but God loves your children more than you do. Your children look to you, trusting you to do what is best for them. Don't let them down.

If you are interested in other fine re-printed fiction
and non-fiction books,
write for a free catalog of all our family building materials.
Mantle Ministries Press
228 Still Ridge
Bulverde, TEXAS 78163
OFFICE: 830-438-3777
E-MAIL: mantleministries@cs.com
HOME PAGE: http://www.mantlemin.com

53

## ABOUT THE AUTHOR:

Recognizing the Providential direction of the Lord Jesus Christ, Evangelist/Historian Richard "Little Bear" Wheeler, through the vehicle of MANTLE MINISTRIES, has integrated his theological and theatrical training to reach believers with a message that will alert, equip, and commission them in their God-ordained responsibility to raise a generation that will uphold the standards of Christ Jesus.

Evangelist Wheeler's approach is to correlate historical facts with Christian influences and tradition and to "re-educate" adults and children via dramatizations demonstrating the spiritual foundations of our nation. Using authentic costumes and props, "Little Bear" (his trade name) presents enthralling portrayals of historical events and stories found neither in public instruction today nor in books published in the last 100 years.

Evangelist Richard Wheeler completed his theology studies at Christian Associates Seminary in Los Angeles and received his ordination to the Christian ministry from Berean School of the Bible in Springfield, Missouri. Prior to his becoming a Christian in 1972, "Little Bear" received music and theater arts training at the Los Angeles Metropolitan Civic Light Opera. He worked in numerous professional productions before entering into full-time evangelistic work in 1979.

Complementing Wheeler's work through Mantle Ministries is his experience as an associate/youth pastor. He also served as an educational instructor with Child Evangelism Fellowship in Southern California. Mr. Wheeler is involved in his local church, Harvest Fellowship, San Antonio, Texas, under the pastoral leadership of Peter Spencer. "Little Bear's" unique and challenging presentations come highly recommended by church leaders and school administrators in 48 states.

Evangelist Wheeler's commitment to public ministry encompasses more than dramatic portrayals, motivational workshops, and keynote speaking engagements, however. He has also founded a publishing organization, MANTLE MINISTRIES PRESS, which re-publishes books written in the 18th and 19th centuries which concentrate on our Christian heritage and Biblical values.

Richard Wheeler married Marilyn on July 29, 1972, and they have three children: Noelle, Aimee, and Joshua. They live in Bulverde, Texas, just north of San Antonio.